Bonny's Big Day

James Herriot

Illustrated by Ruth Brown

St. Martin's Press
New York

One sunny morning in early September, I drove to see old John Skipton at Dale Close Farm since he had telephoned to say that one of his carthorses was lame.

As I got out of the car, the untidily-dressed figure of the farmer came through the kitchen door of Dale Close.

John always seemed to look like a scarecrow, and today was no different. He was wearing a tattered buttonless coat which was tied round his waist with string. His trousers were much too short and, as he hurried towards me, I could see that he was wearing socks of different colours – one was red, and the other was blue.

By working very hard when he was a young man, Mr Skipton had saved enough money to buy his own farm with its handsome stone house. He had never married and because he was always so busy looking after the sheep and cows on the hill, bringing in the harvest from the fields, and picking the apples in the orchard, he had been much too busy to worry about himself – which is why he was always dressed in such very old clothes.

'The horses are down by the river,' he said in his usual gruff
manner. 'We'll have to go down there.' He seized a pitchfork and
stabbed it into a big pile of hay which he then hoisted on to his
shoulder. I pulled my large Gladstone bag from the car and set off
behind him.

It was difficult to keep up with the farmer's brisk pace even though
he must have been fifty years older than me. I was glad when we
reached the bottom of the hill because the bag was heavy and I was
getting rather hot.

I saw the two horses standing in the shallows of the pebbly river.
They were nose to tail, and were rubbing their chins gently along
each other's backs. Beyond them, a carpet of green turf ran up to a
high sheltered ridge, while all around clumps of oak and beech
blazed in the autumn sunshine.

'They're in a nice place, Mr Skipton,' I said.

'Aye, they can keep cool in the hot weather, and they've got the
barn when the winter comes.'

At the sound of his voice, the two big horses came trotting up from the river – the grey one first, and the chestnut following a little more slowly, and limping slightly.

They were fine big carthorses, but I could see they were old from the sprinkling of white hairs on their faces. Despite their age, however, they pranced around old John, stamping their enormous feet, throwing their heads about and pushing the farmer's cap over his eyes with their muzzles.

'Get over, leave off!' he cried.

He pulled at the grey horse's forelock. 'This is Bonny, she's well over twenty years old.' Then he ran his hand down the front leg of the chestnut. 'And this is Dolly. She's nearly thirty now, and not one day's sickness until now.'

'When did they last do any work?' I asked.

'Oh, about twelve years ago, I reckon,' the farmer replied.

I stared at him in amazement. 'Twelve years? Have they been down here all that time?'

'Aye, just playing about down here. They've earned their retirement.'

For a few seconds he stood silent, shoulders hunched, hands deep in the pockets of his tattered coat.

'They worked very hard when I had to struggle to get this farm going,' he murmured, and I knew he was thinking of the long years those horses had pulled the plough, drawn the hay and harvest wagons, and had done all the hard work which the tractors now do.

'I noticed that Dolly was a bit lame when I came down with their hay yesterday,' he said. 'Lucky I come down each day.'

'You mean that you climb down that hillside every single day?' I asked.

'Aye – rain, wind or snow. They look forward to me bringing a few oats or some good hay.'

I examined Dolly's foot and found an old nail embedded deep in the soft part of her foot. I was able to pull it out quite easily with a pair of pincers, and then gave her an antitetanus injection to eliminate any risk of later infection.

Climbing back up the hill, I couldn't help thinking how wonderful it was that old John had made the long journey to see the horses in all weathers, every day for twelve years. He certainly loved those great animals.

A thought struck me, and I turned to him. 'You know, Mr Skipton, it's the Darrowby Show next Saturday. You should enter the mares in the Family Pets Class. I know they are asking for unusual entries this year. Perhaps you should only take Bonny since Dolly's foot will be a bit sore for a few days.'

The farmer frowned. 'What on earth are you talking about?'

'Go on,' I said. 'Take Bonny to the show! Those horses are your pets, aren't they?'

'Pets!' he snorted. 'You couldn't call one of those great big clod-hoppers a pet. I've never heard anything so silly.'

When he got back to the farmyard, he thanked me gruffly, gave me a nod and disappeared into his house.

The following Saturday, it was my duty to attend Darrowby Show as the vet-in-charge. I had spent a pleasant time strolling around the showground, looking at the pens of cattle and sheep, the children's ponies, the massive bulls, and the sheepdog trials in the neighbouring fields.

Then over the loudspeaker came the following announcement: 'Would the entrants for the Family Pets Class please take their places in the ring.'

I was always interested in this event, so I walked over and stood by the Secretary who was sitting at a table near the edge of the ring. He was Darrowby's local bank manager, a prim little man with rimless spectacles and a pork pie hat. I could see that he was pleased at the number of entrants now filing into the ring.

He looked at me and beamed. 'They have certainly taken me at my word when I asked for unusual entries this year.'

The parade was led by a fine white nanny goat which was followed by a pink piglet. Apart from numerous cats and dogs of all shapes and sizes, there was a goldfish in its bowl, and at least five rabbits. There was a parrot on a perch, and some budgies having an outing in their cage. Then to an excited buzz of conversation, a man walked into the ring with a hooded falcon on his wrist.

'Splendid, splendid!' cried Mr Secretary – but then his mouth fell open and everyone stopped talking as a most unexpected sight appeared.

Old John Skipton came striding into the ring, and he was leading Bonny – but it was a quite different man and horse than I had seen a few days before.

John still wore the same old tattered coat tied with string, but today I noticed that both his socks were the same colour and on his head, perched right in the centre, was an ancient bowler hat.

It made him look almost smart, but not as smart as Bonny. She was dressed in the full show regalia of an old-fashioned carthorse. Her hooves were polished and oiled, the long feathery hair on her lower limbs had been washed and fluffed out; her mane, tail and forelock had been plaited with green and yellow ribbons, and her coat had been groomed until it shone in the sunshine. She was wearing part of the harness from her working days and it, too, had been polished, and little bells hung from the collar.

It quite took my breath away to look at her.

'Mr Skipton, Mr Skipton! You can't bring that great thing in here. This is the class for Family Pets!' cried Mr Secretary leaping up from his chair.

'Bonny *is* my pet,' responded the farmer. 'She's part of my family. Just like that old goat over there.'

'Well, I disagree,' said Mr Secretary, waving his arms. 'You must take her out of the ring, and go home.'

Old John Skipton put on a fierce face and glared at the man. 'Bonny *is* my pet,' he repeated. 'Just ask Mr Herriot.'

I shrugged my shoulders. 'Perfectly true. This mare hasn't worked for over twelve years and is kept entirely for Mr Skipton's pleasure. I'd certainly call Bonny a pet.'

'But…but…' spluttered Mr Secretary. Then he sat down suddenly on his chair, and sighed, 'Oh, very well then, go and get into line.'

So John turned and led Bonny to a place right in the middle of the other competitors. On one side of them was the little pink piglet, and on the other side a tortoise. It was a most curious sight.

The task of judging the pets had been given to the district nurse who was very sensibly dressed in her official uniform to give her an air of authority. Judging this class was always difficult, and when she looked along the line and kept seeing the great horse, she knew it was going to be very difficult indeed.

She looked carefully at every competitor, but her eyes always came back to Bonny. All the rabbits were very sweet, the falcon was impressive, the dogs were charming, and the piglet was cute – but Bonny was *MAGNIFICENT!*

'First prize to Mr Skipton and Bonny,' she announced and everyone cheered.

As the rosette was presented, a man came to take a photograph for the local newspaper. It looked as though the great horse knew all about her prize as she posed there, dignified and beautiful. John too stood very erect and proud – but, unfortunately, every time the photographer clicked the camera, Bonny pushed the bowler hat over the farmer's eyes.

It was the mare's way of showing her love, but I couldn't help wondering how the picture would come out.

After the show, I went back to Dale Close to help John 'undress' Bonny – and I went with them down the hill to the field by the river.

As we approached, Dolly came trotting up from the river, whinnying with pleasure to see her friend and companion again.

'Her foot is quite healed now,' I said, noting the horse's even stride.

In the gentle evening light we watched the two old horses hurry towards each other. Then for a long time, they stood rubbing their faces together.

'Look at that,' said old John with one of his rare smiles. 'Bonny is telling Dolly all about her big day!'

Bonny takes first prize in the Family Pets class
(The Darrowby and Houlton Times)